(Cover and overleaf, pages 4-5) Oystermen, James River. Workers on the
James use the traditional technique of tonging to bring in their haul.
(Above) Intercoastal Waterway, Chesapeake.

The photographs on pages 10-11, 12-13, 23, 33, 39, 44, 45, 50-51, 58, 59, 72, and 73
are copyright ©1985 National Geographic Society, and appear with permission of
the National Geographic Society.

The map on page 9 is by Robert W. Cronan.
Redrawn with permission of the National Geographic Society.

Designed by William T. Douthitt and Elizabeth R. Jones
Edited by Carlotta M. Eike
Library of Congress Catalog Card Number: 87-680776
ISBN 0-9616878-9-4

Printed and bound in Japan by Dai Nippon Printing Co., Ltd.

Published by Howell Press, Inc., 2000 Holiday Drive, Charlottesville, Virginia 22901.
Telephone (804) 977-4006.
First edition
Spradlin-Patrick is an imprint of Howell Press, Inc.

SPRADLIN-PATRICK

HAMPTON ROADS

PHOTOGRAPHY BY KAREN KASMAUSKI
INTRODUCTION BY WILLIAM TAZEWELL

Douglas A. MacArthur Memorial, Norfolk. A modern office-building forms the backdrop for the elegant neoclassic dome of the Memorial Rotunda, where the body of the five-star general lies at rest. Although he was born in Arkansas, MacArthur always considered Norfolk, his mother's birthplace, to be his home.

American history began when boatloads of Englishmen came over the water and settled in "Virginia," the land named in honor of Elizabeth, the "Virgin Queen." The homesick English subjects often comforted themselves by giving familiar names to their new homes in the strange land: Norfolk, Portsmouth, Suffolk, Lynnhaven. The names of the Virginia natives whom the colonists dispossessed still remain as well, reminders of the region's Indian heritage: Nansemond, Pamunkey, Kecoughtan (Captain John Smith phonetically spelled it "Kiccowtan"), Nassawaddox, Chesapeake.

The names bestowed upon the region by both colonists and natives reflect the marine influence in the lives of these people. The Indian "Rappahannock" ("the rise and fall of the water") is matched by the English "Tidewater." Formerly the name for the communities on the south shore of the Hampton Roads region, Tidewater and its companion "The Peninsula" (the north shore communities), have been united under the broader designation "Hampton Roads." Since colonial days, the term simply identified the great natural roadstead, but in recent years it has become the more-or-less official name of the entire region that lies near the grand harbor.

While the character of other regions may be defined by deserts or mountains or prairies, the daily life of Hampton Roads, its politics, its economy — its entire history — are to be explained by its waterways. For the first settlers, for example, Virginia's tidal waters were a refuge, familiar and safe in contrast to the savage, unexplored forests. More importantly, however, the Chesapeake Bay and its tributaries were a lifeline — the bloodstream of the colony, the circulation system in a wilderness where there were no roads.

Once the Indians had been subdued or driven inland and the Virginia and Maryland colonies were flourishing, the bay became the aorta of commerce: its capillaries touched the dock of every plantation where a hogshead of tobacco was loaded upon a ship. The export of tobacco — 2,500 pounds in 1616, half a million pounds within little more than a decade, more than a hundred million pounds on the eve of the Revolution — provided payment for the English goods imported to ease the hardships of life in the New World.

"The land was ours before we were the land's," wrote Robert Frost, summarizing the colonial experience. Once the settlers had adapted to their new home, they grew to know their land and prospered in the tobacco trade. Then, when the American republic was realized, the energies of its people turned westward, and the 19th century promised to become the century of the railroad and of expansion inland.

For the inhabitants of the shores where the nation's growth had begun, however, the 19th century proved to be a century of economic stagnation. The boom came to the cities of the fall line, beyond the navigable reaches of the rivers, where the railroads started, while Hampton Roads became a backwater, isolated by the very waters which formerly had guaranteed its prosperity.

The rush to explore America's new frontiers did not exclude Hampton Roads from participation in history, however. Fort Monroe was built early in the 19th century to dominate the region; the Union-held post choked the Confederacy in the Civil War. Here, too, is where the battle of the historic ironclads *Monitor* and *Merrimac* was fought in 1862.

Ironically, the enterprise that crippled the region in the 19th century helped to strengthen Hampton Roads in the 20th century. Entrepreneur Collis P. Huntington established the town of Newport News as the eastern terminus of the Chesapeake and Ohio railroad, and in 1886 started a shipyard there as well. This event, combined with the World War I construction of what would become the immense Norfolk Naval Base, served to transform the cities of Hampton Roads into what they are today: cargo port, shipbuilding center, Navy town.

Subsequently, in the 20th century the region played an active role in America's naval history. From the harbor of Hampton Roads sailed the squadrons of the Antarctic explorer Charles Wilkes and Commodore Matthew Calbraith Perry, who "opened" Japan to the rest of the world.

The Great White Fleet left the roadstead on its round-the-world voyage in 1907 and came home to the harbor in 1909. The next year, Eugene Ely flew his Curtiss-Hudson plane off a makeshift platform on the cruiser *Birmingham* docked here; this first flight from a ship prefigured the aircraft carriers soon to come.

Hampton Roads also saw the 1942 launching of the Western Task Force, which carried more than 30,000 soldiers for Operation Torch, the invasion of North Africa. The Indian Ocean Battle Group returned to this harbor and a tumultuous welcome in 1980 after the abortive attempt to rescue the American hostages in Iran.

The 1.25 million residents of this sprawling naval community live in a patchwork quilt of cities whose boundaries are to be explained historically. The cities of Hampton, Norfolk, and Portsmouth are pre-Revolutionary towns. Hampton is the oldest continually occupied English settlement in America; it celebrated its 375th birthday in 1985. Norfolk was founded by a deed dated 1682 and was the first sizable Virginia town by 1715. It was burned in 1776, rebuilt, and then grew rapidly until the War of 1812. Like Norfolk, Portsmouth was a shipping and trading town. It was named after its British sister seaport, as was the Gosport Navy Yard, established in Portsmouth during the Revolutionary War. It would ultimately become the Norfolk Naval Shipyard (though located in Portsmouth).

Newport News, the result of Collis P. Huntington's entrepreneurial efforts, is home to the immense Newport News Shipbuilding and Dry Dock Company. The yard which Collis established and the Huntington family owned until 1940 is now the largest employer in Virginia, with over 30,000 workers.

The cities of Virginia Beach, Chesapeake, and Suffolk are all newly urbanized counties, formed when the towns of Virginia Beach, South Norfolk, and Suffolk merged with Princess Anne, Norfolk, and Nansemond counties, respectively. They became cities to avoid annexation by their older neighbors. Although born out of a political ploy rooted in the Commonwealth's laws, they are in most other respects boom towns. Each is growing like a teenager, and each has plenty of land that offers growing room yet. Where the architecture dates the neighborhoods in the older cities like the growth rings of a tree, the newer areas are a fairly homogeneous postwar tumble of shopping centers and subdivisions, lapping outward from the city limits of Norfolk and Portsmouth.

The resort strip of Virginia Beach is one of Hampton Roads' greatest tourist attractions; its charms of sand, surf, and sun annually lure tens of thousands of visitors here. "The Beach" holds strong appeal for both domestic and foreign travelers, and it remains one of the area's most magnetic places. The sight of tourists flocking to the shore on a balmy summer day drives home a special point about Hampton Roads: of all the reasons that lead you to the area—to buy a home or take a vacation, to catch a fish or fly a jet—odds are that whatever lured you here in the first place had something to do with the water.

It becomes obvious when you consider Hampton Roads' many sailors—the bluewater sailors of the U.S. Navy, the white-collar sailors who putter about in pleasure craft on the weekends, and the grizzled, vestigial "watermen" who continue to ply the hard and honorable trade of harvesting the water's bounty. The area's economy is dependent, obviously, on the surrounding waters. The building of a nuclear-powered supercarrier or the refitting of a Caribbean cruise ship, the export of coal or import of acres of Japanese automobiles that come rolling off the big ships, the military or the tourism—all reflect the importance of the waters of modern Hampton Roads.

The Alhambra, the great 13th-century palace built in Spain by the Moors, was constructed with a profusion of fountains and pools. The chambers of the citadel abound with light reflected from its pools and echo with the soft murmuring of its running water—a soothing sound to cool and tranquilize the desert kings whose heads burned with the memory of hot sands. It is a temple to the metaphor of water.

Here is a book depicting the life of Hampton Roads and, fittingly, it is indebted in much the same way. As in the Alhambra, you are never far from the water—physically or spiritually. All you need to do is behold the pictures on the following pages to discover this for yourself.

WILLIAM TAZEWELL

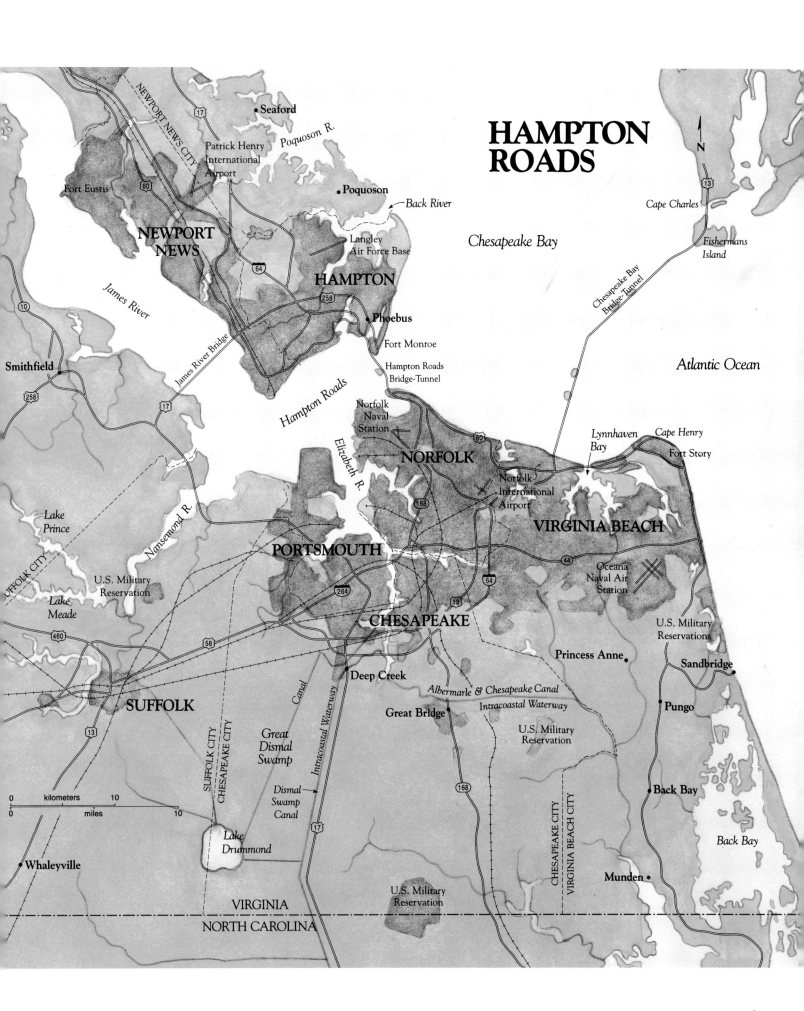

HAMPTON ROADS

N

Chesapeake Bay

Atlantic Ocean

Seaford

Poquoson R.

Patrick Henry
International
Airport

Poquoson

Back River

Fort Eustis

**NEWPORT
NEWS**

Langley
Air Force Base

Cape Charles

Fishermans
Island

James River

HAMPTON

Phoebus

Fort Monroe

Hampton Roads
Bridge-Tunnel

Chesapeake Bay
Bridge-Tunnel

Smithfield

James River Bridge

Hampton Roads

Norfolk
Naval
Station

Lynnhaven
Bay

Cape Henry

Fort Story

Nansemond R.

Elizabeth R.

NORFOLK

Norfolk
International
Airport

Lake
Prince

VIRGINIA BEACH

PORTSMOUTH

U.S. Military
Reservation

Lake
Meade

Oceana
Naval Air
Station

U.S. Military
Reservations

CHESAPEAKE

Princess Anne

Sandbridge

Deep Creek

Albermarle & Chesapeake Canal

Intracoastal Waterway

SUFFOLK

Canal

Great Bridge

Pungo

SUFFOLK CITY
CHESAPEAKE CITY

Great
Dismal
Swamp

Intracoastal Waterway

U.S. Military
Reservation

CHESAPEAKE CITY
VIRGINIA BEACH CITY

Dismal
Swamp
Canal

Back Bay

| 0 | kilometers | 10 |

| 0 | miles | 10 |

Lake
Drummond

Back Bay

Whaleyville

Munden

VIRGINIA

U.S. Military
Reservation

NORTH CAROLINA

9

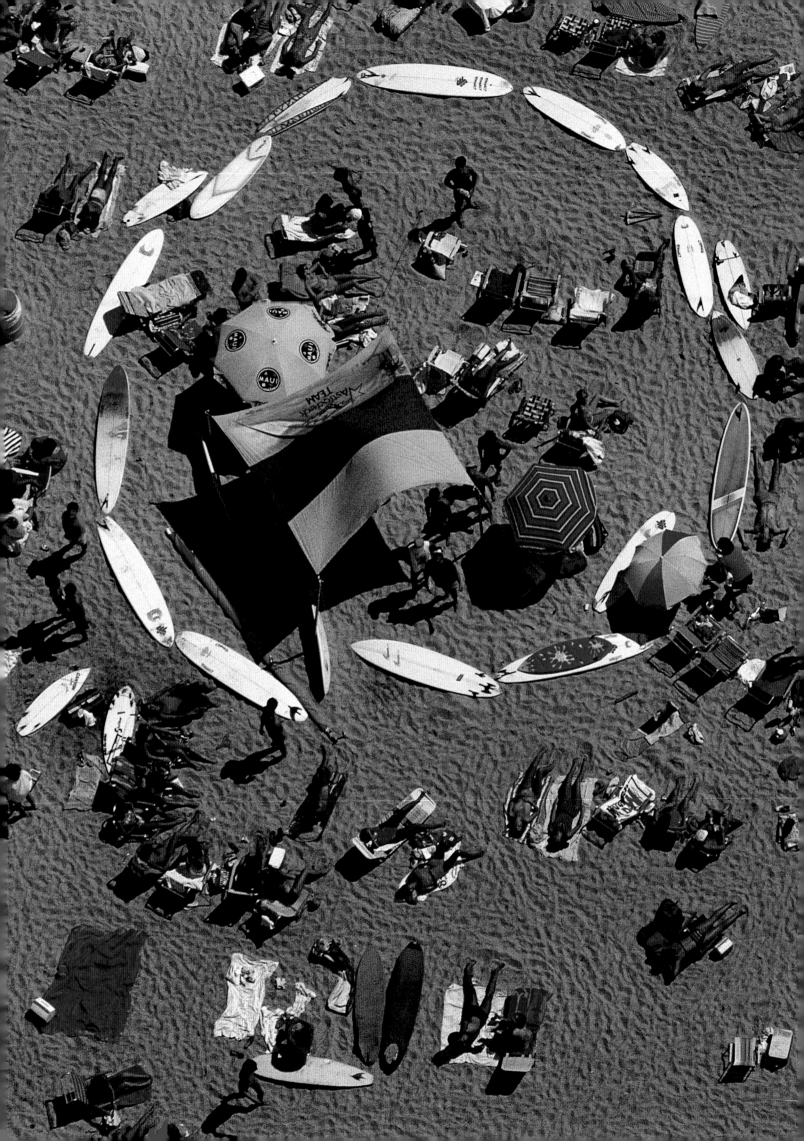

(Overleaf, pages 10-11) Tanker and freighter, Norfolk Shipbuilding and Drydock Corporation. Hampton Roads, where the Elizabeth River meets the James and Nansemond Rivers, is one of the world's great natural harbors. (Overleaf, pages 12-13) Surfing contest, Virginia Beach. In the past, the resort city has been the site of the East Coast Surfing Championship, which attracts hundreds of enthusiasts from all over the United States. (Overleaf, pages 14-15) Fisherman, Great Dismal Swamp. The dense forests and tangled undergrowth harbor wildlife such as bears, foxes, wildcats, and poisonous reptiles. The area is popular with sportsmen and naturalists. Hampton Roads Bridge-Tunnel. Opened in 1957, the four-mile construction links the area's cities, providing several communities with easy access to the rest of the state. Like its 17.6-mile-long companion on the Chesapeake Bay, the Hampton Roads tunnel burrows below the water, allowing ships to pass through the water above.

(Facing) World Trade Center, Norfolk. The center is headquarters for Norfolk Southern Corporation and several
other major corporations. (Above) Sailboats, Norfolk
Harbor. The city's skyline is continually changing. Water-
side, a festival marketplace, opened in 1983.

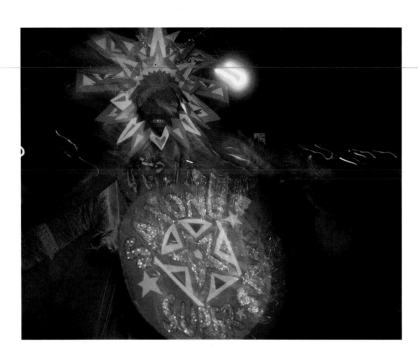

(Facing) Harborfest fireworks. Thousands pack the Norfolk waterfront area during the annual three-day festival in June. (Above) Bahamian band-member, Harborfest.

(Facing) Virginia Opera Guild Ball, Monticello Arcade,
Norfolk. (Above) Opera patrons sometimes find occasion
to dress as characters from their favorite works.

(Overleaf, pages 24-25) Sailboats, President's residence, Hampton University. Founded in 1868 to provide for the education of freed slaves after the Civil War, the school is one of the nation's oldest black universities. Booker T. Washington, founder of Alabama's Tuskegee Institute, is among Hampton's distinguished graduates. (Facing) Concert, Chamberlin Hotel, Fort Monroe. (Above) Bentham Brooks Row, Olde Towne, Portsmouth.

(Facing and above) Adam Thoroughgood House, Virginia Beach. The oldest brick home in America was built in 1636 by Adam Thoroughgood, the settler who is credited with the naming of Norfolk.

Ghent area, Norfolk. Many of the city's stately homes have been renovated recently; several are listed on the National Register of Historic Landmarks.

(Facing) Chrysler Museum, Norfolk. The recently expanded museum is home to one of the nation's top art collections, including the country's largest private glassware collection. (Above) Henry Clay Hofheimer II porcelain collection, Ghent. The Worcester porcelain collection of this businessman and community leader is now housed in the Chrysler Museum.

Gardens-by-the-Sea, Norfolk. Each April, the International Azalea Festival, highlighting the 175-acre botanical garden, honors the North Atlantic Treaty Organization. NATO's only United States headquarters, the Supreme Allied Command, is located in Norfolk.

(Facing and above) The United House of Prayer for All
People, Newport News. Every August the church's mem-
bers hold a mass baptism in a specially built swimming
pool. The day-long event attracts several thousand
participants.

(Facing and above) Residents, Church Street, Norfolk.

Willoughby Beach, Hampton. The busy Hampton Roads Bridge-Tunnel replaced an earlier ferry system. The structure is crossed by 25,000 workers each day and is a vital link for the area's 1.2 million residents.

(Overleaf, pages 42-43) Aircraft carriers, Norfolk Naval Base. The Naval Base
and the Norfolk Naval Air Station together form the largest naval installation in
the world. (Facing) Little Creek Amphibious Base, Norfolk. Naval officers learn
safety in handling full-size ships by practicing on scaled-down models. (Above)
Virginia Beach resort strip. Army soldiers from nearby Fort Story often train here.

(Overleaf, pages 46-47) *U.S.S. John F. Kennedy,* Pier 12, Norfolk Naval Base. Norfolk is home port to much of the Navy's Atlantic Fleet; over 98,000 sailors and marines are stationed in the area. (Facing and above) *U.S.S. John F. Kennedy.*

U.S.S. Chicago, Newport News Shipbuilding and Dry Dock Company. The newly completed attack submarine was the company's 38th nuclear-powered sub. Newport News Shipbuilding is the only company in the country that is capable of constructing nuclear-powered aircraft carriers.

(Facing) NASA Langley Research Center, Hampton. An anechoic chamber at the center allows technicians to test the performance of satellite antennae. (Above) Concepts for NASA's planned space station are tested on the center's models. Langley was the home of the first U.S. manned space program, Project Mercury.

(Overleaf, pages 54-55) F-15 jet fighters, Tactical Air Command, Langley Air Force Base, Hampton. (Facing and above) U.S. Maritime Administration Reserve Fleet, James River. The ships anchored near Fort Eustis await future use.

(Facing) Blue crabs, Hampton. (Above) Fuller's Restaurant,
Phoebus.

(Facing) Chesapeake Bay log canoe, Poquoson. Once a common sight on the bay, the log canoe was the forerunner of the larger dead rise, seen in the background. (Above) Mariners Museum, Newport News. The museum holds one of the world's finest ship-figurehead collections. Its 14 galleries also house carved miniature ships, 50 full-size vessels from around the world, and a library of rare nautical books and maps.

(Overleaf, pages 62-63) Park, Newport News. (Facing) Hampton Roads harbor. The second largest port on the East Coast, Hampton Roads is exceeded only by the port of New York in tonnage handled.

(Overleaf, pages 66-67) Painter, Norfolk Shipbuilding and Drydock Corporation. (Facing) Lamberts Point Docks, Norfolk. Destined for foreign markets, over 40 million tons of coal arrive annually in the Hampton Roads area. The Lamberts Point complex is the largest coal-handling facility in the world. (Above) Portsmouth Terminal. Over 70,000 automobiles are shipped through the city each year.

Peanut Farmers, Suffolk.

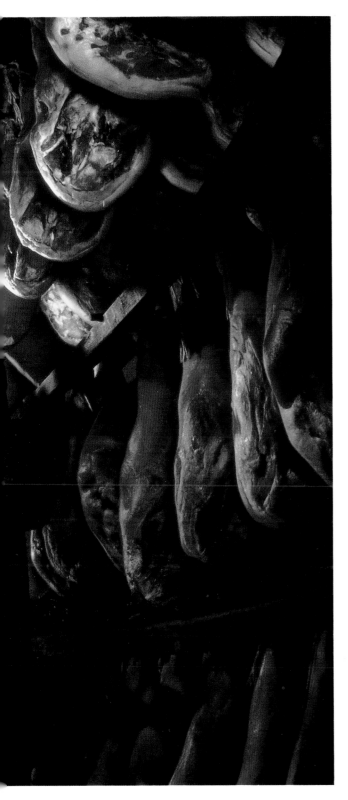

(Facing) Hams, Smithfield. Known for their distinctive flavor, the meats are smoked and aged in the traditional manner. (Above) Peanuts, Suffolk. The Planters Peanuts Company here processes one-fifth of the national total.

(Facing and above) Bergey's Dairy Farm, Chesapeake. Established in 1933, Bergey's is one of the few family farms remaining in an era of rapid development and soaring land prices.

Farm, Virginia Beach. Now the most populous city in the state, much of Virginia Beach's expansion has been into areas that were once farmland.

(Overleaf, pages 78-79) Neptune Festival Triathlon, Virginia Beach. (Facing)
Lighthouses, Virginia Beach. Three generations of navigational aids at Cape
Henry have guided those at sea. Built in 1791, the Old Cape Henry Lighthouse
in the center of the photograph was authorized by America's first Congress.
(Above) Resort strip, Virginia Beach.

Resort strip, Virginia Beach.

(Facing) Sailboat, Virginia Beach. (Above) Kayaker, Virginia Beach.

(Overleaf, pages 86-87) Windsurfer, Virginia Beach.
(Above) Egrets, Back Bay National Wildlife Refuge.